THE KNOPF POETRY SERIES

On Tour with Rita

On Tour with Rita

POEMS BY

Nicholas Christopher

ALFRED A. KNOPF   NEW YORK   1982

3/1984
am. Lit.

THIS IS A BORZOI BOOK
PUBLISHED BY ALFRED A. KNOPF, INC.

Copyright © 1974, 1975, 1976, 1979, 1980, 1981, 1982
by Nicholas Christopher

Poems in this book have appeared in the following publications:
Ascent: "The Driver in Italy," "July 4, NYC," "Room 10"; The Beloit
Poetry Journal: "Big City Glissando"; Cincinnati Poetry Review: "Lord Byron
in Paradise"; Colorado Quarterly: "After the Storm," "Fishing/2," "Three
Poems/2," "Three Poems/3," "On Tour with Rita #'s 2, 4, 5, 16, 17";
Cottonwood Review: "Saturday off Broadway"; Midatlantic Review: "On
Tour with Rita #12"; The New Yorker: "Double Solitaire," "Heat,"
"Nocturne for Miranda," "On the Meridian," "Providence," "Rimbaud
Crossing the Alps," "The Track," "Walt Whitman at the Reburial of Poe,"
"Zeke Mozart's Confession"; The New York Review of Books: "The Road
from Pisa to Florence"; Ploughshares: "Kansas: before the war," "On Tour
with Rita #'s 1, 6, 10, 14"; Pembroke Magazine: "Fishing/1"; Rapport:
"On Tour with Rita #8"; Virginia Quarterly Review: "2 o'clock,"
"John Garfield."
"John Garfield" and "Big City Glissando" also appeared in New York: Poems,
Avon Books, 1980.

Library of Congress Cataloging in Publication Data
Christopher, Nicholas. On tour with Rita.
(Knopf poetry series #8)
I. Title.
PS3553.H75405   811'.54   81-17209
ISBN 0-394-51921-3   AACR2
ISBN 0-394-74998-7 (pbk.)

Manufactured in the United States of America
First Edition

For Constance

Who is the
woman with
us in the
dawn? . . .

H. CRANE

Contents

ON TOUR WITH RITA

SOLOS II

~
The use of this symbol indicates a
stanza break at the bottom of the page.

Solos I

Double Solitaire

Dark, light, your endless equations
From far out of the past,
From rooms where fine music
Hummed the windowpanes into mirrors
And women with waterfall hair (like yours)
Glided, alone with themselves
But with no one else;
I came to your door with a rain-soaked hat,
My ears ringing with footfalls and bells—
As you pointed out, the streets were silent
And there had been no rain for weeks.

Descartes was your god: the man
Who knew that, if lost, one should leave
The Forest by a straight line only;
From the couch, you graphed me against
A dark wall, all points and lines,
Hands, eyes, and feet a jumble of triangles,
Somehow, eventually, a pattern emerging . . .
After supper, after bed, after the last
Of our long silences, I told you that when Dante
Got lost in your Forest he didn't try to leave.
He knew he was on to something.

Heat

The first man in the last
row is waving his arms
so they blur a cleaning woman
listening to the recital by the door.
Someone is saying that time is
a broken shore, more light than rock
except in bad weather. Heat. The raft
with the dangling legs and the polyglot
girls; the meridian shadows—just off-
white; the leaping fish with hearts
compact and cold as lemons; the groves
of unfalling fruit, drunks in the ditches.
A forger is working in a back room
on a bill honoring the General's birthday:
mauve flowers wreathing a sweating horse.
A girl who tends the well
and has never left either of the two towns
(three miles apart) swears she has seen
two moons in one sky, swears also that she never
dreams and that her mother was a Red Cross nurse
who took to a ship's carpenter and jumped
off a roof on Christmas Day, Rio, 90 degrees and windy.
Crashing chords. Rachmaninoff's shadow. The glassblower faints.
Of our dozen strains of blood only two enter
our head and spring into voice—only one intelligible,
melodic, if you want to call it that. Nobody's moving,
everybody's talking. The lone thermometer on the island
runs the Kelvin scale, indecipherable, but hot.
The haze thickens, the flowers remain odorless,
crowds are occupied at their cross-purposes,

their especial preoccupation with the heat
and, after that of course, with sex. A vagrant girl
shimmies clear of her skirt at the well,
the cleaning woman slinks off with a retired carpenter,
no one cares any more about the forger
or the General; there are even two moons in the sky
and even the dreamers see them. The air whirls
green and black. It is finally so hot that nothing
melts, not the ice, not the music,
because that would be impossible.
And that man in the last row is gone now,
before the applause, his shredded program
on his seat, on fire.

Walt Whitman at the
Reburial of Poe

"... of the poets invited only Walt Whitman attended."
JULIAN SYMONS

They got him in the end, of course.
In a polling booth, dead-drunk.
Vagrant, ballot-stuffer . . .
Four Baltimore coppers to carry that meager frame.
Our first detective of the broken heart,
he picked through its rubble
with his frenzied calculations,
his delirium of over-clarity,
until he found too many clues . . .
Once I dreamt of a man on a schooner,
compact and handsome, alone on the Sound,
thrilling to a violent storm,
threaded to this world by the silver
of a dying spider:
that man was Edgar.
He loved the moon, and the night-torch,
the notion of blood sea-temperatured,
of the cold rush impelling him . . .
In life, in poetry, my antithesis—
detached from the true life,
of rivers and birds and swaying trees,
of soil red with tubers and pregnant clay,
detached from the wondrous release of sex,
his spleen beating heavier than his heart—
two or three men (at least)
packed in among a dozen demons.
He never much cared for my work.
I admired only a fraction of his.

But I happened to be in Washington
last night . . . and I'm old now, half-wise,
too old not to have a sixth sense—
for the genuine article, anyway . . .
I marvel at all he accomplished
in such a hatcheted life,
electrifying his losses,
celebrating the deer park, the potter's field,
as I celebrated forest and plain . . .
But then to finish here,
another half-forgotten city,
wearing another man's rags—
a scene he might have written:
streets snaking around him,
steaming and sulphurous,
rain dirty as it left the sky—
one last maze before the foothills of hell . . .
And that polling booth . . .
the drinking pals who dumped him there,
frightened perhaps by that dying wolf's voice;
it strikes me now, the eulogies concluded
(I wouldn't give one and I wouldn't say why),
how appropriate he should go that way,
how perversely American in the end—
a man who had consumed himself with exotica,
green as the Republic itself,
poet of our bloodied ankles and ashen
bones, our cankers and lurid dreams:
I wonder who he voted for.
I wonder if he won.

Nocturne for Miranda

Sky's heavened tonight—
Not for the master, his dome,
His perfect notes off harp-shaped clouds—
Not for any of that,
But for us.
We breathe softly, cross-wise,
A half-murmur, a hundred bypassed
Sentences, and still, things seem clearer
Most of the time.
There are angels everywhere,
Several of them doing imitations
Of us into the twilight,
All of them bright and formally dressed,
Walking the divisions between stars,
Reclining on meteor tails,
High rollers with the wrists quicker
Than light . . .
Now you see them as well;
In some paintings, you say, they glow
Like shadows in a storm:
Ecstatic, grim, never faltering
But always waiting for the fall.

7,000 Miles from Tierra del Fuego

There are fires burning somewhere
I can feel them here in my bed
even their glow
the color of a fox hide
or a rare cactus
their soft crackle, a woman's foot

on the stones the surf has forgotten
the brilliant ones that change
character completely once pocketed
and examined on a night-table
with the rest of the day's debris
cinnabar and jade dulled

the same grey as the turning
waves that smoke out despair
the eye that follows
the progressions of the gulls
through one net and into another
unchastened, bruised, soaring over

those flames that drew us out
of sleep on the verge of yet
another singular discovery
of the chart that brought the island
to us, the glassed oval hovering
in our center, reefed with evasions

~

and loud declarations
coronets sputtering and girls oiling
their limbs in that last thatched
room before the verandah where
we might recline with blistered feet,
cold drink and binoculars to survey

the vista of our lives in allegory
the mess we will somehow make of things
regardless of space speed or pallor
primed like the seals to cleave hoops
and skirt fire, to clap for a fish
and hop the platforms for hire

winter or summer, ice floe or zoo,
unless we emulate the red vine
that outstrips its trellis for a cloud,
attaches itself and sails out to sea
still climbing where the rain
vapors into a sky full of bells,

or with endless cunning
and crisp indifference allow
the hand to make the incision
that will provide us an unimpaired
view of the beating heart,
then all else need not be written off,

~

currents, squalls, inspired navigation,
even the blasphemies an innocent observer
might have heard from our friend
Magellan speared in the shallows
betrayed by still another bad king
and wondering if that island on the strait

with its dusty giants and cliffs of smoke
had not been something dropped from
the heavens to seed another kind of fire
to whirl the white wind black
chasing itself off the map
of sleep, of men sleeping on beds

of coal and ice
and loving it
for no reason they can understand

John Garfield

The heat's on, dead wind shoots up
9th Avenue, flutters the T-shirt
On the convertible's antenna, lulls
The stragglers into Billy's Pool Parlour.
The city's last tough guy
Sidles down 44th Street,
Bumming a smoke, feinting a punch—
Used to show a good left, they say . . .
Later, hat doffed, fingers drumming,
He watches East River tugs
Link the bridges with foam;
Whatever left Brooklyn Harbor
In the last war died, or
Maybe is still out at sea.
After Hollywood, the big money,
The girls with the roulette eyes,
He's blacklisted out of pictures
When he won't give names—
"A matinee socialist," McCarthy calls him.
His voice a hoarseness,
Health gone to hell,
The good looks rumpled into anonymity,
He holes up in West Side hotels
With ex-society girls and B-actresses,
In the end drinks
For nine months straight,
Blacks out regularly at dawn,
Dead at 39, journalists delighted
To report an English girl,

Under-aged and on junk,
In bed with him at the time.

Uptown in a Bronx trainyard
Three kids play blackjack
Under a bridge, blow dope
And belt cough medicine,
Tend a low fire—the fastest one,
In black, keeps losing,
Can't pay up, leans back
And watches rain come down
On a southbound express.

Wasting Away with Passion
in the Luncheonette

Nothing but light. Molasses to peach and then lost
in the sour black corners. Lost as the orbits of
the wood spiders (the fortieth generation) that blew in
between the wars, lost as the flies and the smoke,
a light Corot and maybe Mantegna (that crucifixion-yellow)
would have felt at home in, over ham & eggs,
sipping the first of how many endless cups,
the ballgame on the radio always in the third
inning and the chef, behind his partition, always
straining to hear if the runner tagged up at second
on the fly to deep right, if the relay hit
the cut-off man, and so on, never a fourth inning;
like the storm that never quite made it to sea
and settled, grey torpor and peeling paint, over
the next neighborhood, the row-houses that beg to domino,
the dime-sized lawns, hot sedans, invisible birds . . .
From even the nearest rooftop, tar-slow, your eye
wouldn't catch on this place: glaring window offsetting
the bleached sign, two tables catty-corner to the door
where no one sits, too hot for sitting, the cream
curdled and the shakers reversed, salt gone black
and pepper white, like unmixed dice, permanent
as the silent waitresses, the ashtrays full
of butts, the lottery stubs everywhere.
And the sawdust with its ocean patterns.
And the bad food, steaming.
And the slow fan blurring the clock.
None of that ever changes.
Like the one girl, a quick blonde, who sits alone by the phone.
So beautiful from the back you hope she'll never turn around.

And she never does, though always hovering on the verge
of—not change—but a falling-away from herself:
smoking, spooning sugar, stirring clockwise
that vortex before her stillness, black eddy in the pool,
tapping her foot and filling out her shadow with dry tears
on the dusty floor, within that pregnant dusty light:
the kind of eternity Juliet knew, between her two deaths.

The Track

At the track the horses run
counterclockwise—against time.
In the fields they scatter

around some central idea
which we impose on them.
The thunder breaks differently

on the plateau than on the mountain;
the mice disappear in odd ways,
the owls make contrary moves,

the trees disclose small variations,
but the rain comes in at the same angle
and the wild horses react in the same way—

rearing, white-eyed, under bolts of lightning . . .
Of course all of these horses run
with the clock when they're relaxed.

They connect us to the horizon
with a chain of dust, but too soon
the chain dissolves, the dust settles,

and the wind flies past us, like fire,
into a field which is always empty,
where all the winners go.

On the Meridian

Your feints are choreographed . . .
by the ice.
Cactus crowds the red ravine,
lightning bridges the mountains,
yesterday's sky slides in,
solidifying the props—like definitions:
white table with a pestle,
twin plates of shriveled fruit,
salt rimming a glass.
Sitting back, carnation moon
in your lapel, irises changing
color to a metronome click,
you claim that fog carries
the brighter light, rising
behind you and following the slow
bend that rustles like a river
where there is no river.
The other light is still darkening—
the real moon, a half-moon,
making us see half of what we might be.

Rimbaud Crossing the Alps

He's always thought of as a very young man—
Rightly so. In the mountains, past Gstaad,
He sat in a cherry tree and watched the falcons
Hover after the avalanche, dip, glide,
And return to their masters: men on horseback
In the fast mist. He stayed with the widow
In the house by the waterfall, read her
The single slim edition of his poems,
Verlaine's copy, sent from Belgium,
And this when he was on his way to the East,
When he had given up poetry for a bag
Of maps and compasses, for that deluxe
Money belt from Bern: he was ready for gold.
The widow's thighs went from white to red to snow-blue,
Her pale mirror-image made him wince sitting up in bed,
He mouthed some words when her back was turned,
Saw himself clearly for once: a man just beyond
The glaze of the desert, answering to many names,
Spraying the silence with voices, a sky dense
With suns gangrening his legs, gold raining
Onto his chest, the gold of alchemists
Which he feared in his dreams . . .
The widow stoked another fire, loosened her blouse,
She liked to hear this boy talk, hands
Never still, as she combed out his hair,
She liked his shortened breath and his restfulness
When he fell from her and curled up in the morning light . . .

A few days later, some miles higher,
A man on horseback, mist-featured
And wearing white gloves, found him in the snow,
Half in the blue shadows, out cold, feverish,
And arranged for him to be sent back to France. To die.
The boy was twenty years old.
He would sail east and live another seventeen years.

Salvation Point

My fingers are frosting onto the glass
here at the stone table by the sea
where the chessmen were lost.

On the bluffs, the gentleman in the sunbonnet
plays the Rákóczy March on a hand-organ
for the sunburnt lady in the stetson.

Another isthmus of perpetual off-seasons,
umbrella-less, trackless, no ceramic
nudes or daring noontide surfers.

A place that encompasses the delirium
of Vasco da Gama, the vanity of Coronado,
or the Great Khan hunting with his 20,000 hounds.

But nothing to hunt here.
And only the currents to stalk,
moving away from us, always,

and coming up on us from behind,
under the flat green and sometimes
grey thin clouds rolling off

the horizon like flyers off a press,
ready to be scattered to the dormant
cities, the rooms filled with wind.

~

Speculations about the Milky Way,
the hydraulics of sequoias,
the sonic genius of the dolphin:

nullified here, meaningless as yesterday's tides.
Soon the sun will drop and the moon flash on
and all the white squid tangle into one

writhing mass on the crest of a monster wave,
the myriad fish flung in, and kelp, and shells,
and the empty glass dashed to the rocks, for luck.

Suite for C.

Through the slatted places
even the best light
sometimes falls short
summer or late February when
the sun is most vertical
and we are most prone

to half-dreams, pieces of pieces
silt-grey as dusk and tumbling
leaving us to pick and strum
our chosen instrument (lute guitar mandolino)
at a crossroads as precise in time &
space as the point on the string

depressed onto the point on the fret
a melody of crossroads
which becomes maybe one coincidence

and we're getting louder all the time
star-crazy and dirt-brown
the same description a girl once gave us
of our eyes on the launch cutting
through the lagoon on her way to
excavate something very important

and nearly as rare as our salad
of diced candles and kerosene dressing
the old business of eating the whale
by the lamp of his own oil
except that we plan to consume
light itself with all its accoutrements

~

messy but illuminating, like the boy
who sets fire to the attic of the deserted
house and then slides down a tree to applause

or the rest of us rising with the wind
or with the icy fear there will be no
wind fast enough or slick enough to outrun
that first fire we set, which all through the stubble
of our days has been blackening a somewhat parallel
path, at any moment likely to swerve over

and just like that
there is a morning
of orange hillsides banded
by a silver stream
a dipping wave of foliage
no clouds but only bluer shadows

no trumpet to inconvenience our departure
just some steaming tracks in the white mud,
and a woman at the hotel bar saying

she's always on time in the wrong dream,
and our dim memory of
the bird that flew under
the bridge we were crossing
and reappeared years later
with a fish in its mouth

Levant

The moustached woman puffs her pipe.
The moustachioed man lifts the trembling
girl out of the hammock.
A great cloud of wings rises from the marsh.
There was talk of an assassination
among the overnight travelers
who arrived from the north.
The sun climbed and the mountains disappeared
and the sea was as brown, at its delta,
as the river that runs south from the capital;
when the sea reddened this evening,
those rumors were confirmed.
The birds, already in the next province,
left the mud white and blue
with unhatched eggs.
"Like a second sky," the palmist whispers,
"in which a second cloud will gather, furiously . . ."

2

A slow mist, and a thunder drummed
out by the hearts in the forest,
an exiled matador in the yellow clearing
passing veronicas with the wind—
when he's gored, snow pours from
the cornada and gives a delicate
shape to the wind: a woman
who dances as she melts . . .
While they can, the birds
sip from her shadow with
their short, painted beaks.

The Road from Pisa
to Florence

Orchards and dust, heart-shaped shadows
And upside-down children, the road
A strip of flesh stretched to the sun.
A woman carrying a baby and a sack of mint
Tells us that Cellini, Michelangelo, Raphael,
They all passed this way—it's gratifying
To travel such a celebrated oven: no wind,
Air thick as smoke, clouds bruised into color . . .
In the evening, under a hedge with our grappa
And lemons, we watch the girls in loose white
Dresses, all hips and sidelong glances,
Smiles running like water; suddenly
A dog cuts into a field, the quails rise,
Echoes falter, darkness melts the hills.
My friend, a painter, blacks over his lines
And pockets his pad:
"We never see a place," he says,
"Until we leave it behind." Yes,
And by then it has become someplace else.

Circe

The clarity of Circe
abbess of magic
tangler of souls
force-feeding the swine
their beauty
taking the bravest
upright man famished
and drugging him lighter
than the air he breathes
fouler than the hot
guts that churn inside
his armor
the shapeless clocks
of his mortality
heaped in a wash
of blood
She dangles him
the death living beyond
the wine's frenzy
the poppy's velvet tunnel
beyond the night
that froze the notes
in the discarded flute
the passion he will
abandon on the lip
of the incinerator
Her fervent wish
on her birthday
or any other holiday
in the light-years

of her many lives
wishing to be a lovestruck girl
wishing like a lovestruck girl
to be swept over the cresting
waves on a masculine
wind building to
a hurricane of longing
and consummation
wishing lovestruck to be
a girl without magic
with only the glistening
that overtakes an eye
the prestissimo
that isolates a heart
the lovestruck wiles
that make the flesh genius
for an hour
leaving the others ingrown
in their talky beauty
to perform tricks
with the swine
A labor for women beguiled
by the power without love
that is nothing
To be learned the hard way
like men before them . . .

Zeke Mozart's Confession

Isaiah the weatherman, next door,
Loses himself too much in the geese formations,
The solitary crows. Not me; when I see
The last leaves skid across the first ice,
I get myself out of the woods and into the city,
Search out girls with hotweather limbs
And fired hair, girls with double voices
Who recline on pianos and peel off their stockings
Against a moonlit window . . .
The winter clouds burn blue, they slide
By in the morning, slide smooth as steel,
As if the sky had a light coat of oil;
And me, I'm in the valley driving hard,
Skirting the calm as you might skirt disaster.

Writing Poetry

1

All the lost dramas in the middle-
distance on a spring day.
Blind men playing musical chairs
on a plain where tornadoes
spin sunward like dusty tops.
Quite a thing, that.
As the crossing scales define
the perimeters of the sonata,
so the lattice proportions its shadow,
undulating, on the far wall—
an underwater window, at the mercy of light.
The subsequent definitions of the sea
may be the first in years to touch new
ground, the first in a series of seminal
ratios between light, music, and water.
Like the blond wave breaking
in a field fifty fathoms down,
ringing all the bells in the world
at once: a kind of pure silence
for the unborn.

2

Staring at the thing past himself
(its white hat, from another spring,
boxed and forgotten on a closet shelf),
looking for the glints
that will survive the dousing
of this well-shaped bonfire.
The end of the long roadshow
of the body. That good pal.
Around for so many good years:
soft-dealing the tarot deck
on the edge of the lit marsh;
swimming the night lake twice to
glimpse the daylight in a jumping fish . . .
But who will know what
to make of all these maps
he has passed like a spy in
the summer dusk? Passed through
the hole in the wall that led back
into the same room, to someone else.

Kansas: before the war

They are everywhere in the wild
lights past the hammering of the dawn,
the colors shooting off those sounds,
and she can talk to them, she says,
"communicate" in the same way distant cousins
lean over corpses and say something appropriate
but inaccurate.
Stars cinder where the jungle ends,
at the furthest outskirt of the great
city that false-centers the continent.
The radio is humming between frequencies
and it sounds fine—better than
that last station we heard on the road
about the time she found the dirty map
with the yellow notations she made
on her way to the hospital last year.
This room has two drafts crossing,
one cool, one hot—Bishop B. would have
liked it, sitting up solitary in bed,
but this time my head not his feet.
Outside this hotel is another hotel,
then the zoo, and so on right up to
the burnt cornfield where the mother
of the three-time loser perched on
an abandoned bus in a raincoat soaked
in gasoline and struck a match—
for the good of the country.
Like an act of war, the farmer drawled—
you know, the crazy compass, the boyscoutoath,
fingers crossed just so, and a coin in every mouth—

no, *she* said all that and he shrugged
and a cloud of seeds swirled off his hat
onto our feet.
That's the way it is out here,
not like the curling icewater of our coast,
the green hosannas lost to a roar,
the packed silences . . .
The rickety truck coughs down
the hill road with a load of sheep,
the driver inclines a shaved forehead
like Martin Luther's,
dice are dangling from the mirror,
between them a long yellow jesus—
for luck—
and then it stalls,
rolls to a stop by a creek bed,
more static on the radio but
not a sound from the sheep
as the young man
with the tattooed chest
MY MOTHER WAS A MARINE
jumps off the back
and wades into the white dust,
the steaming skull stones,
looking for something . . .

8.1.78

A fresh sun today,
newly-fired.
And a new sea,
just-flooded.
Even the rocks,
veined back to
the first fire,
the earliest flood,
may have been rubbled
here only last night.
The next island,
snagging the horizon,
breaking that sweet curve,
blurs into focus.
The caiques hover
halfway there, fishing
the fastest channel
where (they say)
the snappers school
by the thousands,
clouds of them placidly
filling the nets.
A girl in black,
white-haired,
climbs the hill;
a widow in white,
jet-haired,
descends it;
somewhere at the crest
they made their switch—

silently, or singing?
Later, the fishermen tell
me all the women
on this side of
the island are named
Kalypso,
"the hidden one,"
and all wear
the same face
unchanging
from birth to death
and back again.

Providence

Those dovetailing heroines with the honey
Tresses, speaking Chinese in hotel lobbies
And crossing and uncrossing their legs in time
To the Pacific Ocean and the end of the world;
Tolstoy had second thoughts about them—
Always *after* the fact—and, personally,
I would not trust them at Russian roulette or religion.

"Rake clear your dreams," she says,
"And realize there is no such thing as
History: it is the miser polishing the coins
He will never spend. Our time here is all
Multiplication and long division, and only
Fools believe you can't divide by zero."
The horsemen drop from their horses without

A sound, swords flashing the sun:
They are in a deserted airport with hangars
Full of holy men, prostrate towards the east,
Carved out of stone . . .
With an umbrella now, she is dancing on a wall,
Waiting for a plane; she is fluent in four
Languages, conversant in all the ways of war;

She likes to read Vico in the bath;
She likes older men.
She calls herself Providence
And insists she's afraid of the water.
A plane appears over the mountains

And the horsemen scatter.
The setting sun revives the statues,

The hangars fill with voices,
She closes her umbrella
And crosses the runway. She waves.
Shots are fired into the air.
Her plane ascends, against a red sky,
And the holy men begin to sing.
The horsemen charge.

Curtain

Why all these delays?
There must be a shadier explanation,
player-piano'd to the kind of jangle
we hear in the dice-throwers' parlor—
something dark, darker than the geometry
of our failed loves, darker even than
our lesser failures, the mirrors we broke
fighting over a girl in the arsoned hotel.
What was sequential, moon-phased, for
our grandfathers, may leave us cold,
probably will in fact—but they too
had their despair: flip-flops with poverty,
uncertain voyages, blunt languages;
not quite the same as all our
airy and complicated labors,
deceit played off with words, lined
with beauty, the varying rhythms finally
more difficult than the life itself.
Which is not to say the onslaught
of what we hear as death is much different
from what they heard, but maybe our particular
echo or pregnant pause (a Doppler effect
ghosting every breath) nudges the calibrations
onto a scale they never imagined.
Two doors down from the whirlwind
the shades take inventory:
all the important things we saw
on this day of our long life,
saw without seeing, without knowing:
silences annihilated with color;

heliotropic gravestones; flying fish
between waves; dusky widows.
We resurrect the after-image of the twin
barrels buckshotting the dammed creek,
a gold spray and mists of unphantomed
swimmers—the full repertory company
of our childhood dreams taking the deep
chilly bow of the endless curtain call.
Cringing in the wings, mouthing
the blown lines, the forgotten cues,
we watch the two extras over their game,
a time-killer, counterpoising in black & white,
finding the calculated error that will be
the victory out of nowhere for one of them;
the rest of us dreaming a scalloped sea
with a plot for everyone, democratic,
the tragic dolphins and the comic shark . . .

On Tour with Rita

"The dreamer is sitting opposite the unknown woman . . ."
C. G. JUNG

#1   Mexico

Busted, throat sandpapered by the wind,
Rita spry as a winter bird rations
The tequila, a shot an hour, ladies first—
She's dreamt there's no water for miles.
Mountains on all sides hazed violet,
Her hair burned gold as the cloud
The hawks halo, a mile up,
Desperate for all their lazy turns,
Scanning the rocks for lizard—
A halo of slashes in a red sky . . .
Rita's restless inside a circle of her
Footprints, squint-eyed and brown, disappointed
That everything surprises her until it happens.

#2   Naxos

Frosted lemon trees, scar-blue clouds,
An erotic sundial in a bare yard:
Out of season and snowy in the hair,
Rita manages a few slow letters and a cycle
Of daily gestures. Once on another island
She left her body well-imprinted
In sand, nestled her bones inside waves
That tossed them like dice . . .
And still, nerveless as a wind
And easily more invisible, she floats
Her idleness on dark seas, travels,
Scatters herself (like a robber hiding booty)
Over a dozen archipelagos and twice as many lovers.

#3   Patmos

Holy men, prophets, twirlers
Of angel lights and sparking scepters—
Words keep all things as one would want them to be . . .
The pomegranate trees, yellow dusk,
Clay mountains circling the bay,
Trapping cross-winds, giving perch
To crazy-eyed men and to Rita:
She's been searching this island
Of the last book for the bloody horses,
The million-blooded sword,
The god, his son, anything—
Now she don't know what's more desolate:
A desert in the eye or an eye in the desert.

#4   Knossus

All pay homage, the thunder claps
And then the thunder is dead.
Rita, limbs of lightning, dances
Faultlessly in Minos' rubble;
Everything is set: the carved crowds,
Wavering moon, delicate winds that ruffle
A gown but leave hair in place—
Oh, Rita, you favored by Apollo after all,
What else did they expect?
In and out of the colonnades
Dart naked girls, pursuers, animals;
Rita's suspended in a pirouette, gold
And divine, prima ballerina of the gods.

#5   Florence

Sun always setting, gold and red
Splayed over the domes, the towers,
The river where women toss their hair
To warm winds like women in a dream,
Women in white, diamond-eyed and apprehensive,
Sharpening their vision on cirrus clouds,
Discarded jewelry and unlit cigarettes
In their hands; Rita, once one of them
Perhaps, now downing Lachryma Christi
And waiting for rain to clear the streets,
Her room overlooking a garden and she,
One part poison, two parts elixir,
Loving flowers like Rappaccini's daughter.

#6   Marseilles

Fishing on the channel, grape-smear
Sky, Rita scanning the tides,
Tamping down the mud with an impatient foot;
Another hour or so and she'll have talked herself
Into thinking there are no fish:
And maybe there aren't . . .
Gulls smudge the mist, currents crisscross,
Kelp tangles, and straight out beyond everything else
The sea angles to the next continent,
A billiard table with lightning bolt cues,
Well-racked ships, and whirlpools neat as side-pockets;
Only whales and 8-balls sit unperturbed,
And Rita, she's still waiting for a bite.

#7   Vermont

Breezes bitter in these hills,
Sunlight avalanching fields
Of corn, insects persisting . . .
Rita there doesn't dislike anything
Except the bats (the white ones) at dusk,
She sits back in dark glasses
Sipping soda water, the dogs
Whining, flattened by the heat.
Come this way with the best intentions,
Virgin notebooks and a bed built
For marathons—she nods off
While ravens with scissor wings
Cut the sky into furling blue sheets.

#8 London

They say comedy is an open parabola,
Tragedy the opposite, upside down,
Zenith & nadir, all o' that;
Hamlet & Lysander maybe meet occasionally
At a common point, some (x,y), you know . . .
Or maybe Rita being just a bit too clever.
Anyway, the stages spin, Billy mentions entrances
And exits: as usual he doesn't miss a trick;
Not at the North Pole, not at the South,
Maybe at the equator, lovely Rita wakes
To find herself spread-eagled (daresay crucified?)
On coordinate axes.
QED, says the doc.

#9　New Orleans

Loud cloud, flood's near, cat
Eating a parrot under the porch,
Bones clattering in the basement;
She wakes every morning tired and dry,
Curtains thicker than night,
Hallway voices brittle,
Hands fumbling at other doors,
Trying keys that never work.
At midnight the clouds bust,
The gulf tide boils,
Two women scream downstairs;
Flood's arrived, Rita's eyes
Lighting up the dust on her face.

#10   Wine

Ever-amazing to Rita:
Vine anagrams to vein
Producing endless nighttime solutions
Of blood and vino.
That erratic half-moon lights
Bloodstreams tangled on a trellis,
Stained hands bandaged with grape leaves,
"Th' future," she mumbles into her glass,
"Is somethin' else altogether."
A bare bulb throws the room
Into sideshow, pipes knock with steam;
All's well—bottle of A-positive in the refrigerator,
Rita's heart pumping a dry Bordeaux '57.

#11   New Year's Day

From the rattle to rattling
Bones—that's neat says Rita
Lying in the snow, hair scattered,
Desert-blonde, out-of-place.
We ride downhill on waxed runners
And never never run out of time
Or snow or night—just breath.
Lungs sop wind, nostrils flare—
But that's not enough.
Even a lover's whistle falls short
When it comes to last gasps.
After the blizzard a man waits
At the foot of the hill,
Feeding the bonfire busted sleds.

#12 Rome

The day comes goes flies,
A dark bird silver-beaked
Circles Rita in and out of sleep,
Sometimes even hovers there in midafternoon . . .
They say some clouds downpour rainbow choirs,
Others blood whiter than rain:
She seems always to be looking for shelter . . .
She asks for a small lull in the din,
A moment of composition, an easy breath;
She's grown tired of the tightrope tonight,
The single luminous razor underfoot . . .
When her eyes—high above—tried
To follow her form into the moonlit garden
She disappeared

#13   Boston

Wonderful that she's surviving
The July evenings, suede hat
Pulled to her eyes, the humidity
So dense it could be raining
And no one would know; her cat,
The one that walks in sentences,
Paws at a mirror in the kitchen
While Rita sprawls out, naked cool legs
On the coffee table, a scratchy Ravel
On the phonograph and vodka spilled
Down her breast; her one open eye
Sees string from wrist-to-ceiling, ankle-to-ceiling,
Then she feels her neck for rope, but nothing yet.

#14   Election Day

Power: the busted vows, the swan songs,
The plummets à la Prospero
And—no surprise—Ariel and his music as
Adaptable as ever for the incoming tyrant;
Our lot to chant while the spoils are divided,
Plutocratic wings unmussed, ink-dark,
And all the vegetation gods dead,
All resurrectees reclined in 'eaven,
No one left to jolt mountains and city-states,
To shake bread from trees, feed
Common slobs, bathe workhorses in wine . . .
When they ask Rita her politics,
She winks and whistles:
"Vote Row Z—Idealist Party."

#15   Route 149

Upstate lakes go pink at 8 p.m.,
June, Rita double-clutching, top down,
Country music coming on strong,
Wind roping her hair;
She gets a freeze in her belly
Seeing the deer lope between pines so
Quickly, their antlers the tuning forks
That hum out the dusk . . .
Not another car in the mountains,
Only fixed eyes and ink-spill shadows;
She pulls over abandoned,
What she'd give for a pal tonight—
This solitude, these pure expanses
Worse than rape.

#16   X

Xmas, x-rated, x-ray,
Xylophones—no, not xylophones.
How many crazy houses opened—
The season has been generous
With tropical monsters and robot snowmen,
Swiss chalets where Dr. X weds
Xanthippe, turns his laboratory
Into a nursery, endures the horror-show
Of domesticity, becomes his own worst nightmare . . .
Xenophobes man the border,
Offer twenty-page visas and bad wine—
The barbarians swarm in.
Rita checks the window for frost, soot,
Webs; the mail arrives,
Her last passion he sends Love & xxxxx

#17   Memphis

Rita Rita sleek as cheetah
Through the bush
Over the gulley
Up the vine—
And straight down again.
Let's not mince it, baby,
The story of the fast cat
Always ends with a drowning.
And a little rhyme.
Not too pretty,
Not too sweet:
Kid sister of Puss 'n Boots
Came to town high-minded, flying,
Hit the road scorch-tailed, crying.

#18   Georgia

Black train flying north, Rita's hat
Awfully large, white-plumed, her
Legs crossed under a cheap novel,
Fingers casual on jade bracelets;
Someone across the aisle snapping
Newspaper pages and swirling cigar smoke—
This game of American spaces can be tiresome:
Trains may pound paradise into honeymoons
And politics, but Rita's bored with the power
Lines, the powder-puff trees on conveyor belts . . .
In a back-station, an unscheduled stop,
She counts seven small boys kneeling in
Sunlight, one of them plucking a dead crow.

#19   Nantucket

She got the shelf stacked
With suicides—Berryman Plath Heming-
way—but, wouldn't you know it, Rita
She love life; she love it bitterly even.
Oh, this no time for maudlin clouds
Or high-floating quotes, no; no peoples,
Poets included, can use the sun for a shield
Nor rain for their private shower:
The things of this world belong to this world
And not to any of us . . .
We finds a watering can cobwebbed and rusted,
We sees a garden full heavy and wet:
Nobody knows what happened.

#20 New York Nocturne I

All right allright alright
Summer solstice, gems falling
From lampposts in the park,
Wolf-moon bright and fast, Rita
Putting her motions in order,
Mouth coordinated to eye, hand
To foot, heart to lung . . . it's easy
But at the same time practically impossible . . .
Twin swans swim circles within circles
On the lake, the symmetrical sky suddenly
Clouds, cold diagonal rain raining
Behind Rita's eyes, beyond the trees;
Moving from one day to another sometimes takes two weeks.

#21   New York Nocturne II

Rita catching some retribution—
That what they call it when birds
Come apart to the eye, feathers
And bones rain down on blithe pedestrians?
She don't know what she done 'cept
A thousand things, hailstorm of guilts,
Ceaseless hurricane of unkind words
And ignored affections; in pieces
To begin with, the life keeps exploding . . .
She ducks into a high-class bar, lots of mirrors,
Builds a pyramid of maraschino cherries
(Red for conscience she nods approvingly)
And flicks them away one by one.

Solos II

2 o'clock

I woke up at two o'clock
in the train station at Trieste,
flat sun and a widow
selling peaches from a sack.
I saw a girl slip through the glare,
a familiar scarf, your easy step,
and enter a butcher shop on the mall.
I asked the conductor, daydreaming,
eating lunch, if he had seen her too,
my lover from California—
he figured I was drunk
and passed me his flask of wine.
When she came out and crossed
the street and I saw that the eyes
were wrong, the mouth not full enough,
I thought, jesus, I'd better move on today,
maybe Venice, maybe farther south . . .
She carried a parcel spotted with blood
and slid into a waiting car beside
an old man who kissed her wrists.
I watched them drive around the corner,
heard the conductor spit on the tracks
and shuffle off the platform.
Then I ripped up your letter.

97 Shadow Street

Unfortunate, the changing weather,
The crowds newsreeled, grey and errand-
Bound, by a distracted eye;
It's springtime and the man on the rooftop
Is dreaming aeroplanes out of another war,
Their soft-drop of spinning
Bombs, one two three four
Neat and green as elm buds
Falling—
Darling,
I can step back only so far
From myself, then it all goes white,
Heat haze over a sea, panels
Of sunlight in an emptied warehouse,
Slide them this way or that
And, still, each square foot is identical
To the last, as it has always been
With the things we have learned to scan:
Meters and horizons, clouded valleys,
Stretches of river between waterfalls,
All of them empty and full at the same time,
Comparable to nothing but themselves—
We can even step back from them
Without making excuses . . .
My most mechanical possession
Thumps in my chest, it is less intimate
To me than the courtyard footfalls
I hear in the dawn, shaving, my tea
Dust-dropped and cold on the windowsill,
The million doves I can summon at will

Crowding my eyes and then disappearing . . .
I am ill at ease
And yet everything seems so calm;
I have a perfect appreciation for hurricanes
And haiku, deserted cities and enameled ikons,
An appreciation for those who juggle mirrors
Behind their backs, who never edge away
From blinding light, who resist transcribing
Their most lucid dreams only to find
Them recurring years later when a sudden
Wave tosses them past some last island,
Into a sea checkered with shadows,
A chessboard of blind swimmers,
The wind moving them until the Queen
Is sacrificed, the King dead,
The wind never dying, the night never breaking.
It is a long way back from there.

Lord Byron in Paradise

for Paul

The idiots, Coleridge dipping into Spanish fly
and Wordsworth mumbling in the woods,
Their kind live to seventy
Taking refreshment in shiny parlors.
I have a room here,
White walls and a blue ceiling,
Foliage painted on the one window—
I exhaust the air with words from time
To time, never write, usually just sit.
They offered me women and I was relieved
To have the *choice*—of course I am alone.
And liquor, opium, wine: all for the asking,
All unnecessary; one point on which I was correct:
Expect no Eden, no Golden Age still-life,
Postpone nothing for this place.
Personally, I'd have preferred hell,
But Minos (a marbled ventriloquist) told me
That those who live fast, not
Pausing for ruts of sleep or comfort,
End up here—why, I don't know.
I'd looked forward to games
Of nightmare and wit, hectic contests—
Instead lounge about, well-preserved,
The trophy of myself on a swept stage.
They say in hell you are doomed to stay;
Here you can always leave,
And that's the problem.

Waking in the Country

First, it is the unfallen snow
the birds are using for a trampoline.
The hint of a rumble in the taut sky.
Then, closer suddenly, the funeral drums
in the next county. The muffled roll
and the shiver of recognition to spirit
fearfully into the past—
another possible revision in the scenario
I have constructed around my own death.
The weather. The city. The voices of companions.

I distract myself: populate the glazed
field beyond the tumbledown wall
with an army of singers, winged
to rise over the trees, to dissolve
in a wave of mist across the mountains.
In the other direction the drums fade
and the dogs bark in unison;
their masters, everyone for miles,
still gathered silently beneath
the single bell that won't stop tolling.

Finally, the snow begins to fall.
Two widows, arm-in-arm, descend the hill
and cross the field in a lazy zigzag.
Overhead, to follow them home, a cloud
of blackbirds has appeared out of nowhere.

Passage

1

The crossed ankles of other men's wives
Flesh marbled just so
The emperor's cats locked in sleep

2

The young girls at the railing
Staring through the spray to the blackened wave
Merging, shimmering, into a single shadow

3

How many clouds to cotton the gaps between mountains
To roll down the choppy glass plain for Africa
Clouds that trick their way onto the map—as continents

4

We pass the same dusky island hour after hour
Sleepy miniature ports with flickering windows
Deserted promenades strung with pennants

5

Another sailor surfaces with uplifted arms
A living buoy to punctuate the currents
Green horseshoe eyes to match the running sky

6

With favoring winds we fear nothing
Not our dreams in the circular rocking of the night
Not the silver glance of the widow stricken with sun

7

Fields of white and blue lilies, of palest anemones
A strayed landscape opens before us on the open sea
The haze-rooted, mist-petaled garden of the sailors

8

Beautiful thieves planted the dynamite under Atlantis
All Anatolia caught the explosion's dust
The gold smoke of the mermaids' palaces, that royal brick

9

In a time before angels, Hermes Messenger was angelic
Winged foot, winged hat, ivory physique
The Thunderer's translator—with a cunning for prophecy

10

Ash clots our wake at dawn
Speckled fish ghost the sea floor
Scavengers seek themselves in endless circles

11

Neat formations dizzy the air
The white-blown wings off seaside trees
Guiding the ships back, either into port or onto reef

12

A woman we know most intimately steps from her bath
Livid hair fanning into the sunset's green
Eyes unblinking our destination, where the sea begins

July 4, NYC

Radios are playing out of unlit windows,
Soft explosions are coming off the harbor:
The astrologers are out tonight in Chinatown
And they all promise to levitate by dawn.
We have parades on every side street,
Novas on every rooftop;
We have a dragon by the tail,
His eyes whirring like cameras,
His heart a ton of dynamite
With fuses into the five boroughs;
We have our Bunker Hill posters
And our taxi drivers from Iwo Jima,
Our burnt-out sparklers and watery beer,
Our nightmares like crimson spoor leading
Back to Seoul and Saigon . . .
Sometimes it's better not to talk.
But not tonight.
The bars are packed,
Sirens are crisscrossing the island,
At three o'clock a last rocket flares
From the Battery, bursts high and pale—
Orchid-shaped, I would swear—and someone
Is whistling a marching song in a doorway.
At dawn I still see the orchid hovering,
Transparent and riddled with stars—
Then it's gone. The crowds thin, disappear,
A man with an empty canteen mumbles
"E plu'bus nullum" up and down the avenue,
And insists that he has it right.

Desire

1

The man of appetite, Balzac or Diamond Jim Brady, casts
his line from the hotel window into the blinking night
and hopes to catch a very big fish. Without fail
he has slicked his worm with a wheeze of encouragement,
crossed his fingers, and told himself which dream to
dream this night—maybe that favorite, again, of the empty
hall with the full banquet, the table set for twelve and he
the lone guest, moving from place to place, delicately . . .

2

There is a sky all of us have seen somewhere,
back-dropping a glance, beyond your everyday blue.
A sky the white of the feather in ice,
of the note caught in the jammed music-box,
of the phantom ship in a pitch sea;
the hypnotic white of the boughed fruit
spinning, as the man's ceiling spins, his sky,
a mix of cheap paint and worse light . . .

3

The forms dancing out of his mirror share a common
fate, all previous tenants who before the glass
admired their flaws and lamented their bad luck,
all swirl around him in a whispering haze
and then slip back, leaving him behind for now,
lost in a vision of exciting black palms and surf
(like lingerie) that unlaces itself with perfect speed,
drawing his eyes out the window, from his bed, wincing . . .

4

Among the many lives it always comes to one,
the necessary connections and currents
rechanneled, passing through the full purgatory
of human desire from boudoir to barroom to bordello,
the life of the invalid masquerading in an athlete's
jersey, a dancer's tights, in the poet's lines which
of necessity spell out the desires themselves connecting:
like the pantomime of the fat man on the edge of his bed

ringing in vain, on principle, for room service,
buttering the wafer moon and sipping tea triple-brandied,
arranging his one dream as he would stock a tank
with blind fish, or design an auditorium for the deaf.

Uncle Joe, 1944

Naples. The soldier-poet. That white sun,
bull's-eye in a silk sky, street-emptier,
traps a thousand pictures in his head,
then boils them free of color, background,
of all human form—
and still they seem cluttered;
the nurse draws the shades . . .
As always, the ceiling rolls,
the walls sway, the windows shrink,
but nothing else changes:
under the enormous bed
the neat pan of blood hums with flies.
One evening as dust pales the shadows,
as the familiar damp drifts in,
he finds himself, finally, with one thought
that has canceled out all the rest;
he will never be sure he wrote it down:

> Everywhere there are things that belong
> in a room but there is no room.

Serenade

From serene. Music with a sky
to reach, a woman to charm.
Rising slowly, like the orchard wind
that carries the retreating voices
of her sisters from the lake.
Come closer, she nods, tossing a smile,
the deep room loosening her from
her dreams of herself: collaged in
flower-and-leaf, half-undressed
on a smoky shell, a jet sea . . .
You play for her all night
and all night she prompts you
with her long looks, her well-spaced
and complicated language, the wine
she doses with clarity and lowers
on a string . . .
Later she guides you
through her window, off the trellis,
nothing more than a rustle and a scent,
and just when you feel satisfied,
heavy-eyed, you catch a disturbing
strain from the garden below—
your guitar, your light touch,
the one song you forgot to play,
the one that will take her away . . .

The Driver in Italy

for David Fichter

Driving, driven,
The driven sun, the sun-
Slicked autostrada, glare
More slippery than ice . . .
Genova to L'Aquila in ten hours,
The day's work a joke
Of wet leather, dusty glass,
Gears caressed with a finesse
Reserved for women
And not a woman in sight . . .
Tunnel after tunnel,
Gutted mountains, dark mileage,
Mussolini's gallerias;
The only art here is the art
Of the foot to the floor,
A crooked arm browning
Out the window,
Chrome of oncoming cars
Flashing bits of the sea . . .
Landmarks never cease:
Here Shelley drowned,
Here Dante strolled,
Here Boccaccio—meanwhile
The scenery flickers
Into a single image
And our bleared eye
Focuses a mile ahead,

Waiting for the driver's
Epiphany, his golden equation—
That moment when he overtakes
An identical sedan and sees,
Behind the wheel,
The back of his own head.

Nocturne in the Year 1997

The black petals in the glass flowerbeds
reflect the irises of the passing nudes.

The stalactites on the 300-story building
catch the lick of flames from an aerial bonfire.

A lonely girl in a blue cape fishes
for amethysts in the rain-filled crater.

This city hovers, the forgotten station
in a dream which last year rocked her sleep.

Let her be the direct descendent of those mermaids
in the curiosity books, fishtailing through evolution.

Let her be the heroine in a dead man's epic,
the survivor of a cataclysm of rainbow weapons.

In the next street the clouds flurry and thicken,
lavender-streaked, drizzling perfumes and dust.

Notched into the dizzying skyline, the dozen shining
balls—once the single Moon—revolve in a figure-eight.

Where trains sped, bodies fly along faster than ideas,
the hot grid of the city running on telepathy.

Murder, baptism, marriage—all ceremonies
climax deep underground, miles beneath the dead.

~

The enormous buildings are filled with saltwater,
piped in from the sea and heated day and night.

Like fantastic aquaria, regulating the development
of the billions of fish into reptiles and then mammals.

An entirely new population to spill into the streets
when these vestiges of the past have disappeared.

The nudes, the telepathic passengers, the dead . . .
and the lonely mermaid, back in her room, drowning in amethysts.

Three Poems

The suburbs were calm.
Red and blue shadows lined the roads.
The barmaid leaned over the table
And had loose change thrown into her blouse;
Come again she said
Laughing, we close at dusk.

Wine, cards, the unpaid check:
His own knife turned back on him,
A twist through the eye and the lights
Of the world suddenly flashing;
The night before, he had walked
For hours and disappeared in a crowd
Where there were no other people.

2 THE KNIGHT

He can only move at right angles.
Sometimes a man, sometimes a horse.
Black or white.
Useful. Short-lived.
Expendable.
If there weren't two of him
He might be King.

3 HISTORY & THE MAIDEN

Rainbows on a steel column,
He dreamt slaughtered legions
Howling on the moon;
After the Games a young girl
Stabbed him in his sleep,
Revolt emptied the city,
But the emperor was a god
And so lived, sailed to Africa,
Roasted meat in the hot sand.

In Rome in the parking lots
There are women who will lift
Their skirts for a thousand lire—
For five thousand they'll get into a car;
The frail seem to have no money
And no luck, the powerful no brains—
Down on the Nile sunbrown girls
Make jewelry from old bones,
Somersault together under naked skies.

The Domino Dance

The reefs begin the domino dance,
rippling gently out into the bay,
a full moon stripping down the mermaids,
fish bones, delicate and clear, ribbed
around human hearts . . .
Underwater the light dies—
Van Gogh's comet escaping
some old sailor's dream . . .

". . . do you mean that someone
threw a flashlight overboard
and the others saw the flying
fish hanging there in the pale
waves like frozen bats and then,
hours later, down on the other side
of the world all the lights came on
in China? . . ." Exactly. Why not?

A gangplank off a balcony on the wing
of a jet, eight miles over the Atlantic
at dusk, a few clouds, a little haze,
a precise circle of sharks below—
like the pool the high diver aims for
in the circus, amid the sea of open mouths
ooohing and ahhhing as he jackknifes twice,
three times, and they swallow him . . .

We're swimming. Back to shore—Spain,
Morocco, Crete? Long golden curve halving
the inside of the indigo balloon.

There's a girl on the rocks,
toeing pebbles, browning, singing
her singsong up through the palms,
about the mermaids, with jangling coral
bracelets, revolving pearl-set eyes,

dancing on their domino graves
to the music of the wafered moon,
an afternoon moon that scales
the mackerel sky and fades away . . .
Through the haze she sees a handsome
skeleton emerge from a tumble of
driftwood, swimming the butterfly,
the surf washing him in silver and

the little rainbow fish passing in
and out of his skull, and when she
swims out to him with an easy stroke,
yes, he even begins to dance,
tap-tapping right on top of
the waters, a mean stutter-step,
back into the darkening bay . . .

Fishing

1 ALABAMA

She leans back, shields her eyes,
July sun emptying the landscape,
Razor stream hollowing the grass:
Time to try again,
So many trout
We can almost hear them
Hovering under the rocks . . .
On our knees, out of bait,
When she pulls a ball
Of worms from the mud, a brain—
She says this water is stocked
With silhouettes and shadows,
The annual rejections of the spring light,
And her brother drowned around that bend.
Later, we leave without a single fish—
We tossed them that ball of worms—
And in the west the heat has thorned
The sky full of punctures;
Cutting through fields,
Detouring the dusk,
"You see," she explains, "they brought
him in and I was too young to know;
when I pressed my face to his chest
the mouth opened, water and blood
flooded my hair . . ."

Canaries, candles, the black
Church flips its shadow from
Street to sea and back—
Quicker than that solitary fisher
Can cast out and reel in,
First a clump of weed,
Then something blue that flops
The gravel at his feet. Lost days.
Dead-glow orchids and salted vines.
A glare that lashes in and in
Repeatedly, flashing the eye away
From the piled reefs, the impossible
Back-swarm of the currents.
The sky rips, as in northern places,
But no rain comes—
Just further ripples of light,
Off the nightmare spectrum,
Unilluminating, black-gold . . .
In the iron hour, the pre-dawn,
Tides out, eyes wind-smeared,
Flesh flickers on the horizon,
Tumbles and flickers again:
For every line that comes out heavy
A dozen others snap on the rocks,
And still another, with luck,
Catches on the shore.

Venus and Vulcan

Like a B-movie.
The bathing beauty and the cripple.
He caught her in the act this time.
With the young fighter, the red-haired fellow.
Threw a net over them, raised a racket.
The neighbors flooded the hallway.
He flung the door open and bawled out his betrayal.
The fighter pushed past him and hurried down the stairs.
His wife huddled under the net, whimpering.
The neighbors gawked and whispered: she had some body.
Despite the scandal, there was no divorce.
She and the fighter continued to see each other for a while.
She won a few contests, he won a few fights.
The cripple kept turning out bric-a-brac in his shop.
When the fighter drifted off, she found someone else.

That's the way things go here on Mt. Olympus.
The gods do their best to imitate men.
It makes the men feel better, you see.

The Amorist's Complaint

—Gracefully I shall cross this room to mine humble bed
and there entertain such notions of ladies long dead,
once loved, as to realign the heavens and brood from
the deaf winds a musical echo—

That's one way of looking at it.
The morning light tossed aside
carelessly with the rumpled sheets,
streaking the poorer objects of the night:

the shattered decanter and crumpled slip,
the wet coat flung over a chair,
the forgotten glove with the crossed fingers,
the pink powder dusting the mirror.

A scene familiar to every Lothario
enamored of the thing itself, for itself,
the spatial agreements (love) rent with forms,
the world an endless sequence of lusts,

a rope of fire spanning steel pillars,
and all of us ropedancers in the beginning
and the end, so many miles to fall, so little sky . . .
Heart askew, eyes aslant, sneaking that second

glance at the morning glory for a revelation
between the amber and the mauve—a mystery;
a second glance into the past reveals
nothing but discrepancies: the eye begging

~

for a window in the hall of mirrors.
I need no glance at all to spy her back then,
bluebirded into shadow, spirited away,
and the rest of them dispirited, arrived

in dead of winter to pick up the slack,
the pieces, to pedestal the fishbowl sun
with its lone barracuda, circling,
bellied full of naked souls and lost hours.

Let's stop there, with the impossible:
the fish that swims inside the sun,
and the lover who left the room
as she entered it—empty and well-lit.

Music

1 THE GREEN SONATA

The themes in the green sonata
cloud the light like pollen,
like gnats sunsetted in July.
There are pianos tumbling
on the bottom of the lake,
bumping in the trees, pianos
pedaled as furiously as bicycles.
No one can play the piano
that rings with the green sonata.
Maybe it will play forever
in some hidden corner of the woods,
behind a curtain of vines,
paler, more intangible, than a shadow.
Maybe it is filled with rain,
or with birds nesting after
a continental migration.
As always, it reverberates
the uneasiness, the finality,
which music shares with silence,
the many themes circling back on themselves;
on certain nights, unrecorded,
something requiring no piano at all.

2 EARLY MORNING

Vivaldi's is the music of sweet defeats,
of a gap in the burning hedge that divides
the darker counties of the mind, left and
right, right and wrong, writing our florid
confessions by a speckled light, under the high
ceiling the bodies smack into like mud
on their way—where?
Our sculptor knows, with his locust
inspiration, his iced palms and humming lip;
he marshals his forms with a flick of the eye,
takes no commissions and needs no references.
His assistants, up from the river, rain-masked,
cross the plain every night and chip at the rim
of the city until finally it collapses inward—
the body-politic into the melting heart
that lavas over the empty lots and hardens:
the final evolution of sculpture.

Island

The burning bush spins down the cliff
But there is no sea below;
It burns all night.

The coyote is eating blackberries,
Fish are jumping the dunes,
A September sun glazes the daffodils,
And the people pray for rain in a time
Of floods, for a rain syncopated and oblivious
As an army of drummers.

Here, at noon, you can pocket time
Like a candy, or a precious gem—
Everything is crystallized, even your ideas.
You will find women lolling in
The dust, or smoking scented cigarettes
In the plaza, but none of them will speak

Any language you understand, none
Of them will even know what you want,
Regardless of your gestures or your hungry looks;
Everyone likes to sleep alone except those few
Who are married to each other's shadows,
And they don't sleep at all.

In the days of the volcanoes
Women lived in pairs and the men
Tended the animals and the corn;

There were no priests or temples;
Ships without cargoes came and went regularly;
For a century no children were born

And the leopards hunted peacock
In the suburbs. Bowmen descended from
The mountains one night, and at dawn, miraculously,
A schooner appeared, crewless, white, a hundred
Virgins sunning on the deck. They began again,
And gradually the leopards were killed off.

The night is edged with phosphorus,
The beggars are moaning for softer music,
A meteor the size of the moon
Is passing unnoticed out over the bay,
And in the casino that doubles as a cathedral
A robed croupier twirls his wheels of fire

And never says a word. Only the women can
Gamble (a throwback), but spectators of all sorts
Jam the balcony, toying with abacuses and
Signalling to the floor. Later, they are given tea
That makes them desirous of snow; they can imagine
Nothing else; finally they are ushered out.

A young couple from the mainland—stowaways off
The midnight ship—swim across the channel and linger
Over the skyline, all green glows and powdered winds;

They speak in singsong phrases that clatter
On the air, they steal fruit from an orchard
And begin to dream of circling leopards—

So quickly that they are not aware of having fallen
Asleep. At daybreak a sailor finds them trying
To set fire to the sea. They are wearing leopard skins
And they have arrows through their hearts.
Above their heads, on a cliff,
A bush has just burst into flames.

After the Storm

Gone, the moon gone,
The yellow weeds that sway
By the road, the stars that tumble
Across the lake at dawn;
I been in & out, up & down,
I been clearly out beyond the parade,
At the far reaches of the parade's music,
A girl there, silk-eyed, presented me
With a necklace cold off her chest,
Cold and too bright.

The big house was locked,
At dawn all the windows were closed,
The grey light in the front hall
Shadowed the coat rack, the umbrella stand,
The same girl. In white with a striped ribbon.
She was holding a shard of glass monocle-fashion,
Her feet were smoldering—not on fire—
And there was something dazzling
About the way she tossed her hair
And rolled her eyes and never spoke.

Saturday off Broadway

Oh sugar, them buildin's
is growin' humans outta windows
wit' real hair an' wide open moufs—
but even when they talk in their sleep
no one believes them.
The wind is heavy with smoke
and scent, you wear your papery dress,
your smooth-as-glass smile,
and over Jersey the clouds
accumulate, nightfall approaches,
eased on with grey oil
but still a little scratchy—
like a cheap watch . . .
I come in after midnight
and find your sister asleep
in front of the television,
hands translucent as fish,
her shadow working the far wall,
somewhere in the past
and very busy.

Two Dreams at the Hotel Argentina

1

The women in the other dream
walked a bridge of lightning
from pole to pole. Thunder
filled the rooms in the sky
and a lavender shadow drifted by
on the heels of a two-legged wind.
No one tried to sing on the ledges
beside the waterfall.
The more talented orphans sped
through their lessons-in-love
and emerged triumphant,
even high-principled,
but they had no secrets
to share and, in the end,
the women they skirted
and the women they bedded
troubled them equally, using
the same harmony in different songs.

2

What might best be remembered
at this late date, between
the solstice and the red-hot ice,
is the scent that blew over
from the hair of the women
on the far shore (the place
where the sea goes), where
volcanoes are ranged with all
other varieties of passionate peaks,
snowed, sapphired, and universally admired;
best remembered in the threatening
fashion of a train roaring
alongside the flimsy walls of
deep sleep, a train filled with women
against a cold, fire-colored sky,
entering some other dream through
a tunnel of silence cut into the mountains—
an instant before the explosion.

Room 10

"The elegant woman died staring
out the window and was illuminated
by lightning as he broke
through the door . . . "
She closes the book with a grimace
and wets her lip, trying to picture
the volcano we passed yesterday.
The wallpaper keeps moving on me,
dark blue, with stars the color
of sour milk.
The fan on the table is too slow,
chopping the air like gravel—
as if, even outside our dreams,
we're trapped in stone.

Once, from the flank of the acropolis
at Lindos, I saw a ladder of orange
spiders drop from the clouds and
Aphrodite herself naked, dripping pearls,
descend with amaranth eyes in which the surf
was breaking gently, inward . . .
I wrote postcards that night
until my hand ached,
and each one the same:
—Sea indigo. Towns geometric.
   Athens t'mw.
   Girls everywhere—
It's always been that way—
talking around myself, soft-pedaling,
one ear to the crowd . . .

It happened I returned to Athens
not the next day but the next month.
I met a girl on the quay with a parrot
and an umbrella, traveling with her cousin,
nameless, asleep back at the hotel;
late that night the cousin and I
sailed for another island together.
In Athens, meanwhile, nothing had changed:
I looked down an alley to the Tower of Winds
and a white cat leaped overhead, window
to window, as a woman screamed with delight
in the first window and the dusk dropped
a shade . . .
It was there we went our separate ways;
the film in my camera—
which I remembered as all
flowers, churches, ruins—
turned out to be twenty shots of her,
overexposed, that I lost somewhere
between Byron's statue and my hotel.
Then I put myself to sleep reading
this same book, with its dead women
and lightning—
of course I couldn't mention that now, here . . .

I've been up all night again,
conjuring beautiful storms,
searching those stars for constellations—
and finding too many.
On Friday I bought my postcards,

only two, identical,
that we're using as bookmarks.
For a long time nothing happens.
Then the first clouds dust the sky
and she turns again, clockwise
against her sleep,
like the spider that just spun past
the window, across the sun,
glowing . . .

Birthday Poem

Turning the corner on the bright blue shadow,
But never losing it—its solitaire glow,
Always a step away, stalking us, repelling
Light, E-ternal as the island trees
That screech with cicadas . . .

After so many steps it seems
As if no step has been taken;
Clouds, heavy and too white, fleet the sky,
Fast birds unstitch the landscape, roses blur:
In the last year we has reaffirmed
That the lives of men is flimsy things,
Kindle for the heart's bonfires;
In the last year we has made our calculations
And way-stationed our lovers,
We has heard too many voices at midnight,
Too much music at noon . . .

From the other end of the street,
Late in the day,
A man approaches carrying a mirror,
Trying to reflect light onto his shadow,
Carefully, up where the eyes would be.

Seascape

Outoftheblue
the night
when the flowers open
to the sea
wind glassing the waves
that carried the cargo
of blindfolds in
from the wreck
one morning
a year or two ago
maybe even before
any of us were born
under these same low clouds
that drift in raining sand
lashing the tree-line
until the fear of the desert
comes over us
fear that the moon
will light only a pile
of bones
for each of us who
might try to skirt
the shadows searching
for a way out
before the night ends
the closing petals of
desire
breath
dawn that will never expand
into noon

a sky where birds never pass
where something else takes flight
disappears into a distance
blue thickening
past black
shards pieced together carefully
where the sea should be swelling

The Soloist

I like black doves.
On the last day of the month
Two women knocked at my door
And had identical knocks;
They were not sisters,
But they also came and went
With the same words.
This may happen again,
Next month, next year—
It's all one to me . . .
The lowest clouds bring the most rain,
The loveliest face always catches the light;
As a boy, I fished near the blackberry bushes:
They put you to sleep, and that was often
Convenient—like the zodiac.
I was born Fish (sign of), I caught
A trout once in my life,
In a burning haze,
And the line snapped.
Of course only a man
Like Odysseus would swim
Hundreds of miles for a woman,
Only an accomplished liar;
I like women to swim to me
And I like to swim circles
With them—gently—circles that end
With a clean underwater thump.
I clearly remember a girl
Fingering my spine on
The hillside, the first time,